Don't

be

so

Pernickety!

Don't Be So Persnickety!

The Runaway Sneezing Poems,
Songs and Riddles
of
John B. Lee

Illustrations by
Frank "Woody" Woodcock

Black Moss Press
2000

Published by Black Moss Press 2450 Byng Road,
Windsor, Ontario N8W 3E8. Black Moss Press books are
distributed in Canada and the U.S. by Firefly Books.

Black Moss Press acknowledges the generous support of
the Canada Council for the Arts as well as the Ontario Arts
Council for its publishing program this year.

Acknowledgements
"When Witches Walk Widderships Against the Sun" first
appeared in the anthology Sing and Play Special Days by
Denise Gagne.

Canadian Cataloguing in Publication

Lee, John B, 1951 —
        Don't be so persnickety

Poems.
ISBN 0-88753-352-3

        1. Children— Poetry. 1. Title

PS8573.E348D66 2000   jC811'.54   C00-901180—3
PR9199.3L44D66 2000

Cover illustration by Frank "Woody" Woodcock

for Cathy and Mr. Two Boys

Contents

viii

Don't Be So
Persnickety!

The Runaway Sneezing
Poems, Songs and Riddles
of
John B. Lee

Illustrations by
Frank "Woody" Woodcock

Dilly Wakeup and the Runaway Head

One blustery Saturday morning
When I didn't go to school
I was lying in my bedroom.
I was feeling like a fool.

I reached upon my shoulders
But there was nothing there.
I couldn't find my nose nor ears.
I couldn't find my hair.

I sat up in an instant,
Leaned off my old bunk bed
And there, lying on the carpet
Was my ears, my nose, my head.

It was quite an awful sight
That I couldn't almost see.
Me almost looking down at *it*
And *it* looking back at me.

I gestured to my ear lobes.
I gestured to my nose.
I gestured to my open mouth
And what do you suppose?

It leapt up from the floorboards.
It leapt up on my neck.
I pushed it down and held it.
It shouted, "What the heck!"

And now this silly head it stays there
Upon that neck of mine
Because I have it fastened
With some string and baler twine.

Hairy Man

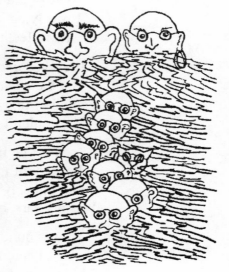

I knew a man
and his name it was Stan.
He had hair all over his chin.
Yes he had a long beard
and it looked real weird.
He had hair all over his skin.
      Hairy man
         Hairy man
         Hairy man.
He had a wife
and he took her for life.
She had hair all over her face.
Yes, she had a long beard
and she looked real weird.
She had hair all over the place.
      Hairy woman
         Hairy woman
         Hairy woman.
Now, they had seven kids
with hair all over their faces.
Seven hairy hairy kids
with hair in the strangest of places.
And they had long beards
and they looked real weird.
      Hairy kids
         Hairy kids
         Hairy kids.
They lived in a hairy house
on a hairy hairy street
and they had hairy neighbours galore.
But the hairiest of all the hairies

was the hairy Harry who lived next door.
And they all had long beards
and they looked real weird.
They had a hedge hog
and they had a hairy dog
and they had a hairy hamster too.
They had hairy cats
some hairy this and thats
they even had a hairy gnu.
And they all had long beards
and they looked real weird.

    Hairy pets

           Hairy pets

           Hairy pets.

    Hairy neighbours

           Hairy neighbours

           Hairy neighbours.

Young Stan he was saved
one day when he shaved
all the hair from off of his face.
But it still looked weird.
It was just as I feared.
His face it was just a disgrace.
So he has a long beard
and he looks real weird
but at least when he goes for a walk
he has a long beard
and he looks real weird
like everyone else on his block.

           Hairy man

           Hairy man

                Hairy Stan.

I Loved a Little Lily

I loved a little lily
living lonely by my house,
a lovely tiger lily
living right beside my house.

His throat was orange.
His spots were black.
I want my tiger lily back.

He grew outside my kitchen door.
He isn't with me any more.
My lily caught a little cough.
The winter came and froze him off.

His throat was orange.
His spots were black.
I want my tiger lily back.

What Rhymes with Orange?

Of all the fruit upon the tree
I'm glad I am an orange.
But if you squeeze
Out all my juice
I'll squeak just like a door hinge.

Riddle the First

Always talking;   Always moving;
Never speaking.   Never walking.
Always looking;   Always listening;
Never seeing.   Never hearing.

Bless my wooden little head.
What am I?

Puddle Hopping Boy

I met a puddle hopping boy
while on my way to work.
He was hopping into puddles
as if he'd gone berserk.

He was splashing to his ankles
to his middle, to his ears.
He was splashing past his haircut
till his hat had disappeared.

Now I wondered if his mother
and his father would agree
with when I hopped along beside him
and he hopped along with me.

8

How Billy McPuck Almost Died Because of a Knee Injury

Bonny & Johnny McPuck-in-the-knee
and Billy McPuck-in-the-head
were having a game of shinny with me
And Sally O'Mally and Fred.

And Fred slapped the puck with a high stick
so it flew like a bird in the air.
And Billy McPuck, so down on his luck
took the biscuit right under the hair.

So Johnny & Bonny and Fred
And Sally O'Mally and me
Said, "Billy McPuck, are you dead?"
As I leaned on his chest with my knee.

And to Johnny & Bonny and me
and to Sally O'Mally and Fred
said Billy McPuck, "Can't you see!
If you don't lift your knee, I'll be dead."

Riddle the Second

Old lady's bones
up!
Old lady's bones
down!
Old lady's bones
where I knit, knit, knit.
Old lady's bones
where I sit, sit, sit.
      What am I?

If Friar Tuck
Were a Fire Truck

If friar Tuck
were a fire truck
he wouldn't a friar be
but a fire truck
named friar Tuck
is very fiery.

And if friar Tuck
put a fire out,
would a fire truck
put a friar out?

Riddle the Third

I can't be told.
I'm seldom bold.
I'm sometimes old.
If you say me
I'm not me
any more.

What am I?

Oh Walk with Me to the Sea

Oh, walk with me
to the sea by the sea
at the end of the sea by the sea
and we will see
what we see
when we see
the sea by the sea
at the end of the sea
by the sea.

Oh, she
walked with me
to the sea by the sea
at the end of the sea by the sea
and we saw
what we saw
by the sea
by the sea at the end of the sea
by the sea.

And we stood
where we stood
as you stand
where I stand
and we saw
what we saw
by the sea at the end of the sea
by the sea
as you see
what I see
as you stand

where I stand on the strand
by the sea at the end of the sea
by the sea.

Understand?

We saw sand where we stood
as we stood on the strand
by the sea at the end of the sea
by the sea.
We saw sand.
We saw sand.
We saw sand where we stood
as we stood on the strand
by the sea at the end of the sea
by the sea.
We saw sand.
We saw sand. We saw sand.

Understand? We saw sand where we stood.
as we stood where we stood. Understood!

After Dark When You Walk Alone

When tickle rain is coming down
With shadow people all around
And trees are making "sussing" sounds
You know it is the night.

The breeze is wheezing through the leaves.
The graveyard graves are grieving grieves.
The moon believes what it believes
By giving all its light.

You walk with "click click clicking" feet
Down a once familiar city street
But waving shadows that you meet
Are hiding out of sight.

The rain comes down so prickly damp.
It drizzles under each street lamp.
But on and on you tramp, you tramp
First looking left then right.

This is your family neighbourhood
Which, earlier today, was good.
But let it now be understood
It's giving you a fright.

For after dark, when you walk alone
The shutters knock, the houses moan
And shadow people steal your bones
Because it is the night.

When tickle rain is coming down
With shadow people all around
And trees are making "sussing" sounds
Until you're out of sight.

Breakable Man

While I was walking down the lane
I fell down and broke my brain.

    While I was walking in the air
    I fell down and broke my hair.

While I was walking on a pier
I fell down and broke my ear.

    While I was walking in the sky
    I fell down and broke my eye.

While I was standing by a rose
just to sniff it I suppose
I fell down and broke my nose.

    While I was walking on a farm
    I fell down and broke my arm.

While I was standing on a pig
I fell down and broke my lig.

    While I was standing on a cow
    I fell down and broke my brow.

While I was standing on a bull
I fell down and broke my skull.

    While I was visiting the south
    I fell down and broke my mouth.

While I was walking underneath
I fell down and broke my teeth.

While I was walking with a pup
I fell fifteen stories up.

    While I was walking with a cat
    I fell down and crushed my hat
    Imagine that! I squashed my hat.

While I was feeling quite cantankerous
I fell down and broke my pancreas.
Yes I was feeling like a lummox
I fell down and broke my stomach.

    While I was lying still in bed
    I fell down and broke my head
    leastwise that's what my mother said.

I fell down and broke my head
leastwise that's what my mother said.
        And that is why I'm here in bed.

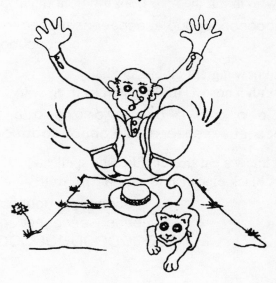

When Witches Walk Widdershins Against the Sun

ooooooooooooooooooo
eeeeeeeeeeeeeeeeeeeeee
oooooooooooooooo

I knew a man without a head
When it was Halloween he said

oooooooooooooooooo eeeeeeeeeeeeeeeeeeeeeee
oooooooooooooooo

I knew a ghost, oh what a fright
When he came out that October night!

ooooooooooooooooo eeeeeeeeeeeeeeeeeeeeeee
oooooooooooooo

I knew a terrible ugly witch
Who drank the mud from my front ditch!

oooooooooooooooooo eeeeeeeeeeeeeeeeeeeeeee
oooooooooooooo

I knew a giant all big and hairy
With a nose THIS long and teeth so scary...

o o o o o o o o o o o o o o o o o o o
eeeeeeeeeeeeeeeeeeeeeeee oooooooooooooooo

I knew a cat that could cast a spell
A black black cat in a deep dark well!

ooooooooooooooooooooo
eeeeeeeeeeeeeeeeeeeeee
oooooooooooooooooooo

I knew a skeleton all bones with no skin.
He'd rattle his ribs if you ran into him!

OOOOOOOOOOOOOOOOOOOOO
EEEEEEEEEEEEEEEEEE
OOOOOOOOOOOOOOOOOOO

I looked at the moon in the moaning wind.
I looked at the places where lanterns grinned.
I looked at the sky with a witch on her broom
And I'm glad I'm at home in my own bedroom.

(*softly*)
oooooooooeeeeeeeeeeeeeeeeeeeeeoooooooooooooooooo...

When Snowmen Thaw At Night

I built a snowman
On my lawn
But when I woke up
He was gone.
   His head was froze
   His body cold
   He stuck together
   When I rolled.
I built him slowly
And with care
With sticks for arms
And grass for hair.
  With stones for eyes
  And crooked nose
He stood there
On his frozen toes.
He stood there quite
As tall as me
For he was made
Of snowballs, three.
I thought he was
My special friend.
Oh why does winter
Have to end?

Riddle the Fourth

I live in a box
with an *old crank*.
And if she turns on me
I JUMP!!

Backwards Running Dog

My dog runs backwards
Down the hall.
Sometimes she's big.
Sometimes she's small.
Sometimes she isn't there at all.

She says sometimes
that life is "Ruff!"
That trees are made of "Bark!"
and stuff.

She plays guitar
with both her paws.
Sometimes she plucks it
with her jaws.

My dog runs backwards
down the stairs.
Just like two tumbling
teddy bears.
She lands and slides
across the floor
then scrambles backwards

out the door.

Don't Be So Persnickety

When I was but a little lad
and mother was my mommy,
she worried quite a bit about
what I put in my tummy.

Eat your broccoli; eat your beets...
And don't be so persnickety.
Gobble up your fatty meats
your bones they won't be rickety.

I know the butter has been churned.
It's yellow soft and runny.
I see the bacon's stiff and burned,
but the eggs are white and sunny.

So don't be so persnickety.
The milk is warm and creamy.
The cow is standing in the barn
her eyes so large and dreamy.

Swallow up your vitamins
and gulp the oil of cod.
The winters here are very long
And though the food is odd...
Oh, don't be so persnickety
and do eat all your vitals
Boiled apricots are good for you
and so too are the skittles.

I've chewed potato's sprouted eyes
I've eaten fruits that I despise
I've swallowed apples Dad called spies.

I've noshed the carrots hairy knuckled
the parsnips bent, the garlic buckled
the mushrooms that my uncle picked
turned black and watery and thick
and even though they made me sick
I chewed my food
and swallowed hard.
I'd eaten every fungus
my mom put on my plate
because
the portions weren't humungous.

I wasn't so persnickety
I never got bone rickety
And if you find me pickety
From eating things too thickety
It's just because I'm sickety
Of being non persnickety.

Riddle the Fifth

My daddy was a dinosaur.
My mommy was a bird.
I start with "**p**"
I end in "**t y l**"
Oh, what a silly word.

What am I?

How Doth My Little Crocodog

How doth my little crocodog
Dare grow so gross on scraps?
She drinks up such a healthy grog
Of water poured from taps.

She's like a cushion, old and gray
And sat on getting flat
Because she lay about all day
So lazy, wide and fat!

Riddle the Sixth

I carry what I bury.
What I bury is not dead.
When I don't bury what I carry
then, I dig it up instead.

What am I?

Jerk Gerbil

Jerk is a gerbil
living in my house.
He looks a little
like a hamster
and a little
like a mouse.

My grampa doesn't like him.
Nor does my mother's mom.
But I love him. Yes, I love him
Though he nibbles on my thumb.

Ebenezer the Sneezing Dog

Ebenezer is a dog
With a funny sniffle.
He sneezes when he's standing.
He sneezes when he's down.
He sneezes through his nostrils
With a wh-wh-WHIFFLE!
    So-o-o-o, I say—
Ebenezer!
Heavy Sneezer!
Where'd you get that NOSE?
Ebenezer!
Heavy Sneezer!
Sneezed off all his TOES!

Ebenezer is a canine
With a strange suspiration.
He sneezes while he's dreaming.
He sneezes while awake.
He sneezes with his mind
Upon some canine concentration.
    So-o-o-o, I say—
Ebenezer!
Heavy Sneezer!
Where'd you get that LUNG?
Ebenezer!
Heavy Sneezer!
Sneezed out his long TONGUE!

Ebenezer is a Cur
With a Cur's KERCHOOS!
He sneezes in the parlour.
He sneezes in the den.
He sneezes all his dog food
In his master's work shoes!
    So-o-o-o, I say—

Ebenezer!
Heavy Sneezer!
Where'd you get that TAIL?
Ebenezer!
Heavy Sneezer!
Sneezed his head into a PAIL!

Ebenezer is a pooch
With a vicious cold.
He a-choos in his supper.
He a-chews up his lunch.
He a-choos when he's very young.
He a-choos when he's old.
        So-o-o-o, I say—
Ebenezer!
Heavy Sneezer!
Where'd you get that AIR?
Ebenezer!
Heavy Sneezer!
Sneezed out all his HAIR!

Ebenezer, dear old hound dog.
Ebenezer, dear old pup!
What you breathe in
What you wheeze in
You're always sneezing up!

So, I hope
That in the next life
If a next life
There might be
You'll get a doggy nose job
One that gives you sneezing peace
Cause the one you got in this life
Makes the sneezing never cease!

Bowling with Gerbils

My gerbil bowls at pop cans
In his rolling bowling ball.

He knocks them
where I set them
when I set them
on the floor.
He rolls across the kitchen
and out the kitchen door.

He rolls across the carpet
He rolls across the rug.
He scoots across linoleum
Just like a beetle bug.

But if you would go bowling
with your gerbil anywheres
Don't call him from
the main floor
when your gerbil is upstairs.

B
     u
             p
       m
              i
                 y
               t
                  b
u
          p!
m

Riddle the Seventh

I don't mean
to ALARM **you,**
but there are bees
in my pants.

bzzzzzzzzzzzzzzzzzzzzzzzzzzzzzzzzzzzzzzzzzzzzzz!!!!!

What am I?

Oh, Penelope Penelope My Penny Hamster Dear

Oh Penelope Penelope
sweet hamster in my hand.
If I should squeeze
and she should squish
I hope she understands.

It's not that
I don't love her,
my Penny Hamster dear.
It's that she's such
a squeezy thing
to squish beside my ear.

And if she's smaller
in the belly
than she is at either end
while I squish
like apple jelly

Penelope, my friend

I'm just a boy,
a little boy.
Perhaps I should know better.
But if I dared
to set her down
my cat might go and get her.

Jack Black, The Cat Snack

My boy he brought a gerbil home
The gerbil was my boy's.
He put him in his bedroom
in a cage among his toys.

He named the gerbil Jackie.
Yes, he named his gerbil, Jack!
Until the cat came in the room
and had a gerbil snack.

"I want my gerbil Jackie!
Yes, I want my gerbil Jack!"
But when a cat is snacking
you can't have your gerbil back.

Yes when a cat is snacking
upon your gerbil Jack
the cat who is attacking
will have his gerbil snack.

The moral of this poem
Is sad and it is true.
The cat who eats a gerbil says,
"I'll have another two."

Herman Head Cheese: a gerbil's tail/le

Mr. H. H. Gerbil Cheese
if you wish it, if you please
chewing at a toilet roll
like a mousie
like a mole
makes a paper-feathered nest
where he takes a little rest.

Master Herman, Master Head
sleeping in his little bed.
Mr. Gerbil, H. H. Cheese
on his tiny gerbil knees
chewing, chewing every night
just to get his bedding right.

My Skunk Stinky

I had a stinky skunk
and the stinky skunk stunk.
He lived down in the basement
by my grandma's cedar trunk.

My uncle tried to trap him
in a box below the stairs,
but he sprayed my stinky uncle
when he caught him unawares.

So now my uncle's stinky
and my house is stinky too.
Oh, it's stinky! Yes, it's stinky!
Whew, it's stinky! P.U!

The Awesome Opossum in My Back Yard

A possum digs things in my back yard.
His butt is soft; his nose is hard.
His face is long; his tail is scaly.
He sniffs into my garbage daily.
My brother and I both stand and stare
At his sharp snout and his gray hair.
His jaw is white; his nose is pink.
Part rat, part coon, part pig, I think.
A brave and bold and slow marsupial
We watch him eat from our back stoopial.

The Polly Ester Parrot & The Dust Ball Dog

The polyester parrot and the dust ball dog
slept all day inside the shoes I wear to jog.

The vacuum cleaner snake
and the dressing mirror sheep
tried and tried all afternoon
but couldn't get to sleep.

The pink puppet pig and the stuffed brown cow
were not sleeping either
though I think they're sleeping now.

The blue bear, plum bear, sugar bear bears
stayed up for seven hours
now they're fast asleep upstairs.

So if you plan on staying
awake for several days—
Be quiet as a Kleenex
or a mouldy bale of hay
cause they're sleeping, oh they're sleeping
for how long I cannot say.
And if you must be noisy
please go outside to play.

Riddle the Eighth

A lady sits down
in a chair.
And so, the chair
is warm.

An hour
She's been sitting there.
She will not
come to harm.

Her knitting
it falls on the floor,
the chair
it goes cold.

and then a knock
comes at the door
to tell her
she is old.

Who is she?

El Gecko the Painting Lizard

El Gecko was a skink
with a paint brush in the sink
and a portrait on the wall
in a clay bedappled hall.

He was feeling kind of Spanish
though he wasn't very mannish
for a lizard so artistic
and a prehistoric mystic.

He drew his flicking tongue in
when he was but a youngin'
and there was an insect on it
with two wings that buzzed upon it.

That was his first bug dinner.
Yes, he was a late beginner.
Yet when he became a master
and he hung things on the plaster
They called him Great El Gecko
though his art it was not deco.
It was scaly, slither taily,
kind of squeamish, squished and screamish.

Now, he's famous as a blizzard
this imaginative lizard
and he's gone and gorged his gizzard
with some flies.

But he's left his art quantity
to some tsetses in the city
so he'll get a little pity
when he dies.

Sean-Paul's Wish

I wish I had a lion,
a furry jungle cat.
I'd dress him in pyjamas
and a funny little hat.

I'd tuck him in at bedtime
where he would sleep with me.
But if he bit me in the night,
I'd punch him in the knee.

My Parakeet Pete and My Canary Harry

My parakeet Pete
and my canary Harry
were sitting on their perches
feeling quite contrary.

My blue parrot Gerette
and my cockatoo Lou
were squawking in their cages
for an hour or two.

My love bird Bert
and my cow bird Gert
were pecking on the buttons
of my father's plaid shirt.

So I opened all the windows
and I opened all the doors
and all my birds, they flew away
by twos and threes and fours.

The Awful Big Mosquito That Bit My Dear Old Dad

In the hot and steamy jungle
Through the tangle of the plants
Comes the hungry Armadillo
Looking everywhere for ants.

Then sliding through the waters
That feed the river Nile
Comes the scaliest of killers—
The ferocious crocodile.

Or slithering through the branches
Where monkeys rule the trees
Comes the whispering anaconda
As silent as the breeze.

While down to drink the water
From the sweetest of lagoons
Come the leopard; come the tapir;
Come the thirsty brown baboons.

And high above the vultures
Circle in the air
While the jaguar and the lion
Groom their tongue-licked hair.

From the Congo to Malaysia
To the Mighty Amazon
From New Guinea where it's rainy
Till the rainy season's gone

From Indo China, Indonesia
To the forests of Brazil
Where the toucan eats bananas
With his multi-coloured bill

There's no creature quite as awful;
There's no creature quite as bad
As the awful big mosquito
That bit my dear old dad.

Riddle the Ninth

I'm a lively little fellow
With a lively little brain.
If you go without a shirt
I will light on you like rain.

ZzzZ
   Z
       ZZZZZZZZ

Z
   ZZZZZZZZ
ZZZZ
      ZZZZZ ZZZZZZZZ
ZZZZ
           z
   z

What am I?

Mosquito Mosquito

Why do you bite?
Singing and winging
All day and all night.

I slap you.
I clap you.
I squash you to black.
And still you come

   still you come
   still you come back!

Polliwog Polliwog Tadpole Frog

Polliwog polliwog tadpole frog
sittin on a lily pad. Sittin on a log.
Maybe it's the springtime
April, May or June.
Maybe it's a summer night
Underneath the moon.

Breezes on the water top
singing in the reeds.
Croaking old amphibians
swimming through the weeds.
Puffing out their mating call
for some passing ear.
Bullfrogs falling quiet
when I come too near.

Will I bring a jam jar?
Will I bring a pot?
To keep these black spring peepers in
when a few I've caught.
Will they sprout some legs and feet
while I keep them cool?
Will they turn a deep deep green
and hop about my pool?

Now I'm getting older too
with hair upon my face.
I have to shave it twice a day
if I go any place.
But every spring I think upon
those tadpoles in the pond
wriggling there like fishes
round and round and round.

Maybe I'm an old man
Maybe I'm a lad.
Maybe I'm a young girl
out there with my dad
lying down and dreaming
watching them swim past
polliwogs and tadpoles
growing up too fast.

Polliwog polliwog tadpole frog.
Sittin on a lily pad. Sittin on a log.
Maybe it's the springtime
April, May, or June.
Maybe it's a summer night
underneath the moon.

Pond Song

Once I was a beaver
with a beaver wife.
We sawed down trees
and chewed on twigs
without a paring knife.

Yes, we built a dam
and lived there
all our beaver life.

Amoeba! Amoeba!
   My tiny little fellow.
   If there were enough of you
   You'd turn the water yellow.

I have a paramecium
swimming in a jug.
I can't see him,
But it must be him
he's such a little bug.

Ladybug, ladybug
my pink and black beetle
will you sit upon my palm
and stay there just a little?

I'll love you
and watch you
and make you a home.
Then neither of us
would be left alone.

Glowworm, lightning bug, firefly, come
like stars in the grass in the night without sun.
Bring your bright little bodies to flash in the black
where you carry your lanterns lit up on your back.
Blink on and blink off, o'er the pond in the willows.
Blink on and blink off, my merry young fellows.
Carry galaxies down to me where I rest
For wishing on fireflies is what I like best.

Crabs and crayfish
Mites and snails
and little snapping turtles
with pointy mouths
and pointy tails
and hard shells just like girdles.

Perhaps an army
has its ants
I know I have them too.

I felt them biting
in my pants
and crawling in my shoe.

If a mantis prays
    and a dragon flies
    and a bee will bee all day.
Why then my daddy
    has long legs
    to keep the rain away.

Lady harpist pluck each strand
or ride a raindrop to the ground.
Eight long fingers for a hand
your instrument, it makes no sound.

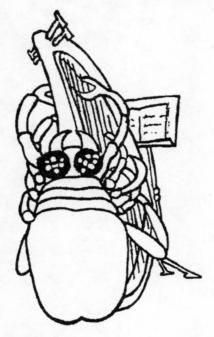

If a fungus
were humungus
the way a pig
is big
why then a mush
would be a room
where you could dance

Pumpkinseed sunfish
swimming in the water
bite the worm upon the hook
to say my daughter caught her.

If the bulrush rush
to heave a scythe
for the bull rush matador
who takes the swamp
with blade in hand
to cut away the shore.

If toads don't sit
on toadstools
and cat tails
have not cats
why where then do
the toads sit
and where then
are the cats?

A heron sat
beside a snake
and said,
"There must be some mistake.
You just crawl,
but I can fly.
And I look better

       The snake he made
a quick reply.

Said the snake unto that bird
"SSSSSSSSSSSSSSSS may be my only word.
My tongue be forked.
My head be flat.
But my body's slim
while yours is fat!"

"You may fly
while I but crawl.
You may be big
while I am small.
Yet stood on end
I'm rather tall."

The snake he hissed.
The heron cried.
The snake he slithered
side to side.
The heron ruffled
up his wings
and flew
then said,
"That's more than you can do.

"Yes, true
I'll stay a snake
I guess
and crawl upon the ground."
And so he hid
beneath some leaves
and made
no further sound.

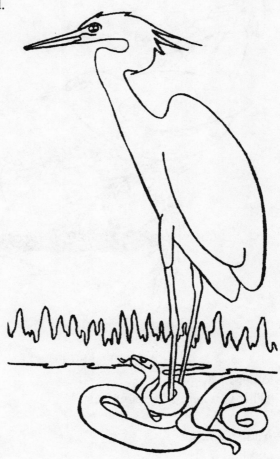

Said the marsh wren
to the goose,
"I know where you have been.
I've seen you flying from the south
though you'll fly back again.

Said the blackbird
to her nest,
"This is where I lay eggs best."

And so she sat
and laid a few
just the way all blackbirds do.

I'm a duck
and I'm a pike
and I'm a lily pad.

I'm a fly
a dragon fly
just like my dear old dad.

I'm a carp
and I'm a bass
and I'm a bottom feeder.

And I'm a tiny
little worm
tied to a hook and leader.

Bull frog! Bull frog!
Calling out so deep.
When you croaked
my family woke
and couldn't get back to sleep.

Bull frog! Bull frog!
Ribetting in the water.
With a puffed-up throat
for a deep down note
you've looked for a mate and caught her.

Bull frog! Bull frog!
My *Rana catesbeiana*
I look for you'n
the dark flat tune
of my grandma's old piana.

Bull frog! Bull frog!
My large brown and green cold blooders.
Your young polliwogs
they swim between logs
And grow up to look like their mudders.

So here I sit a thinking
beside the beaver pond
Of all the plants and animals
I'm really very fond.

I come here every spring
to watch the frogs unfreeze.
To feel the wind. To see the leaves
Unfolding in the trees.

I like the bugs and fish and birds.
I like to look for nests.
I like the snakes and dragon flies,
but I like the beavers best.

Riddle the Tenth

Albert Norman Onymous
Didn't know his name.

He asked,
Who am I?
Who am I?
Who am I?

Albert Norman Onymous
asked his mommy dear.

He asked
What's my name?

What's my name?
What's my name?

Why doesn't he know?

Riddle the Eleventh

There is blood
      in my cupboard
      and
I think I'll drink it soon.

By the way,
for those of you quite puzzled,
my favourite actor
is Jack **WEBB**!

What am I?

Riddle the Twelfth

I hold a tree
Below my cap
And I'm a little squirrelly.
In winter time I take a nap.
But in the spring
I wake up early.

What am I?

Riddle the Thirteenth

Listen!

Do you hear it? No?

Why not?

Because it's never truly there.

What is it?

Riddle the Last

Who am I?
Of all the snowflakes in the sky,
Of all the sand upon the shore,
Of all the water in the sea,
Of all the starshine in the night,
Of all the dust within the blue,
Of all the people in the world,
Who am I?

And who are you?

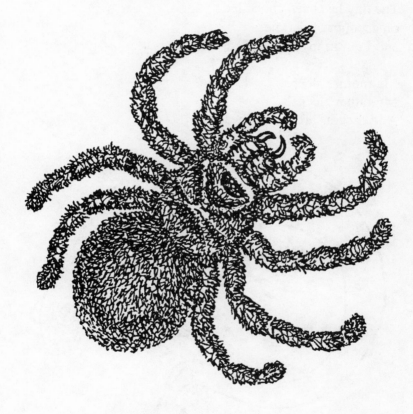

Cancelled on Account of Darkness

The day has been cancelled
on account of darkness
and I am in my bed.

My mother sleeps.
My father sleeps.
And dreams are in my head.

Answers

Be very careful in answering riddles that you don't con-
fuse the answer the author had in mind with the one that
might be the best answer. Often authors are wrong about
the riddle of their own work.

So, if you must always be right, then answer "Tarantula"
and you will always have the right answer. If you would
have the best answer, try this riddle written by a child and
learn.

> I am round.
> I am silver.
> I go down the stairs
> very wild.
>
> What am I?

If you said, "a slinky," then you have the answer which
the author had in mind. If you said, "your grandmother
when the house is on fire," then you have a better answer
because: grandmothers are sometimes round when they are
plump, they are sometimes silver when their hair is white,
and they certainly go down the stairs very wild when the
house is on fire. So, try John B. Lee's riddles and have
fun. Say, "Tarantula," say something interesting and fun
because as long as it fits, the fun is in the trying.

author's answer

Riddle the First   a marionette
Riddle the Second   a rocking chair
Riddle the Third   a secret
Riddle the Fourth   jack in the box
Riddle the Fifth   pterodactyl
Riddle the Sixth   a squirrel
Riddle the Seventh   an alarm clock
Riddle the Eighth   shadows at the end of day
Riddle the Ninth   a mosquito
Riddle the Tenth   anonymous
Riddle the Eleventh   a spider
Riddle the Twelfth   an acorn
Riddle the Thirteenth silence
Riddle the Last   myself

AGMV Marquis

MEMBRE DU GROUPE SCABRINI

Québec, Canada
2001